PREVENTING ASTHMA AT WORK

HOW TO CONTROL RESPIRATORY SENSITISERS

HSE BOOKS

© *Crown copyright 1994*
Applications for reproduction should be made to HMSO
First published 1994

ISBN 0 7176 0661 9

CONTENTS

Introduction 1

The problem of occupational asthma 2
How does it develop and what are the symptoms? 2
Long-term effects of sensitisation 2
What causes sensitisation? 3
Extent of respiratory sensitisation 4

The law requires . . . 5
Complying with COSHH 5
Adequate control and exposure limits 6
Practical advice on controlling respiratory sensitisers 6

Advice on complying with the Regulations 9
Regulation 6   *Assessment of health risks* 10
Regulation 7   *Prevention or control of exposures* 12
Regulation 8   *Use of control measures* 14
Regulation 9   *Maintenance, examination and test of control measures etc* 16
Regulation 10 *Monitoring exposure at the workplace* 18
Regulation 11 *Health surveillance* 20
Regulation 12 *Information, instruction and training* 22

Annexes 25
1 Substances responsible for most cases of occupational asthma 26
2 Some other substances reported to cause respiratory sensitisation 27
3 Sample questionnaire for screening employees working with respiratory sensitisers 28
4 References and further reading 32

INTRODUCTION

1   This guidance gives you practical advice on how to protect your employees from the ill effects of 'respiratory sensitisers'. Respiratory sensitisers can cause permanent damage to the nose, throat and lungs. Once sensitised further exposure to the sensitiser, sometimes to even tiny quantities, causes allergic symptoms. These range in severity from a runny nose and watery eyes to asthma which, on occasions, can kill.

2   HSE estimated that in 1992 there were over 1000 new cases of asthma caused by exposures at work[1]. In addition, about 70 000 people in the UK believe that they have asthma caused, or made worse, by substances breathed in at work[2]. This makes respiratory sensitisers a major cause of occupational ill health. For many people development of respiratory sensitisation results in permanent lung damage; breathing difficulties continue long after exposure to the sensitiser has ended.

3   Many different kinds of substances may be respiratory sensitisers - chemicals, metals, and natural substances of animal or plant origin. Turn to Annexes 1 and 2 for further information.

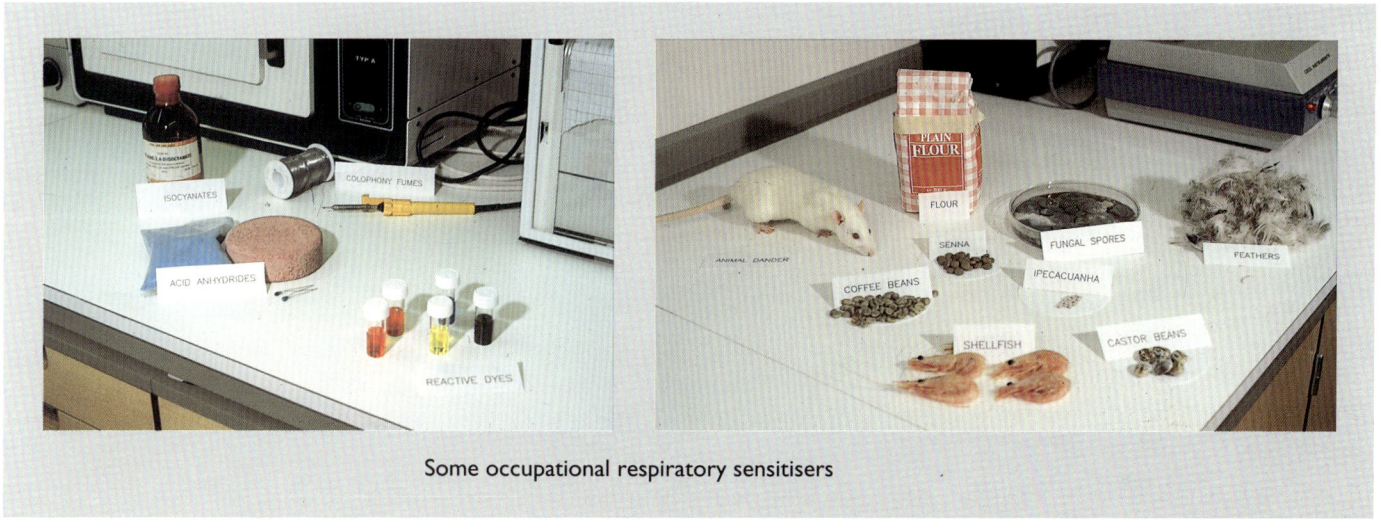

Some occupational respiratory sensitisers

4   If your work activity involves any of these substances and your employees could breathe them in, then you have legal duties and should read this guidance. It gives:

- an explanation of respiratory sensitisation;

- a list of common respiratory sensitisers;

- the legal requirements imposed on employers to protect their employees; and,

- practical advice on meeting these requirements.

THE PROBLEM OF OCCUPATIONAL ASTHMA

HOW DOES IT DEVELOP AND WHAT ARE THE SYMPTOMS?

5   Sensitisation is a result of changes to the immune system which normally protect the body from the harmful effects of contaminants in the air we breathe (for example, microbes or 'bugs', dust). It is different from many other forms of toxic effect because it is 'all or nothing' (the person either becomes sensitised to the substance or does not). Sensitisation is:

- substance-specific - symptoms initially occur only in response to that substance;

- unpredictable - only some individuals at risk will become sensitised, typically 5 - 25%;

- latent - sensitisation may occur after months or even years of exposure;

- irreversible - although symptoms disappear when exposure stops, they may reappear if exposure occurs again, even after several years;

- but sensitisation will not occur once exposure has stopped.

6   When a worker is sensitised, allergic symptoms may develop on any re-exposure. The symptoms are:

> **Asthma** - periodic attacks of wheezing, chest tightness and breathlessness resulting from constriction of the airways;
>
> **Rhinitis and conjunctivitis** - runny or stuffy nose and watery or prickly eyes, typical of hay fever.

Rhinitis, conjunctivitis (and sometimes dry coughs) are the most common effects of sensitisation and may lead to asthma if further exposure to the sensitiser is not stopped.

7   The symptoms either occur immediately on exposure or after several hours. If delayed, they are often most severe in the evening or during the night, so workers may not realise that it is work that is causing the problems. However, if they get better during weekends and holidays they may begin to suspect.

8   Symptoms develop at much lower levels of the substance than those which first caused sensitisation and well below levels which cause other harmful effects.

LONG-TERM EFFECTS OF SENSITISATION

9   If exposure continues, symptoms are likely to become increasingly severe:

- People with rhinitis may go on to develop asthma.

- Attacks of asthma are likely to become worse. Once asthma is established attacks may also be triggered by other things, such as tobacco smoke, cold air and exercise. Such attacks often continue for years after exposure to the sensitiser has ended.

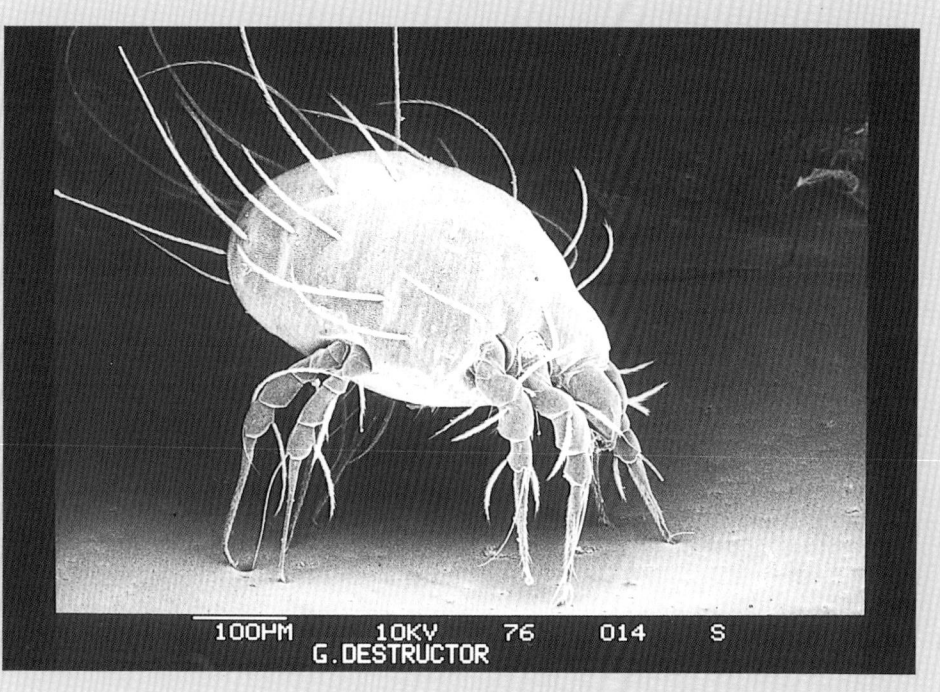

Storage mite - a close relative of the house dust mite. Both are respiratory sensitisers

10 Some people who develop occupational asthma become so disabled that they cannot work again. Most have to change to a job where they are not exposed to the sensitiser. They may no longer be able to use their specialist skills and may face a cut in pay. A few people die from slow deterioration of health caused by occupational asthma. Occasionally, a sudden severe asthma attack results in death.

WHAT CAUSES SENSITISATION?

Extent and pattern of exposure

11 The main thing seems to be the overall amount of exposure to the sensitiser. High exposures over short periods and long-term exposures to lower concentrations may cause sensitisation. No-one can predict if one sort of exposure sensitises quicker than another. Most people who become sensitised do so during the first two years of exposure, often in the first few months, but sometimes it occurs after years or even decades of exposure.

Activity of the sensitiser

12 Different substances do, however, sensitise at different concentrations. Some will sensitise below one millionth of a gram per cubic metre (equivalent to a few specks of dust in London's Royal Albert Hall). For other sensitisers the level needed is considerably higher.

13 It is difficult to find out how much exposure is needed to cause sensitisation. To do that you need to know:

- how many workers have been sensitised;

- which substances have caused the sensitisation; and

- the extent and pattern of exposures of the workers to the sensitisers, over say, the previous five years.

A good deal of research is going on to answer these questions (some of it funded by HSE). But it will be some time before we have the data to show what is a 'safe' level of exposure for the main sensitising substances.

Existing respiratory diseases or allergies

14   If workers already have respiratory disease or breathing difficulties their chances of becoming sensitised may increase and their symptoms may become more severe.

15   About a third of the UK population are estimated to be sensitised to common environmental sensitisers, such as grass pollens, house dust mite and animal dusts. Such people are said to be *atopic*. Only some of them show allergic symptoms, such as hay fever. Atopic people may be more readily sensitised to natural products but this difference is not evident with manufactured chemicals.

16   Since atopic and non-atopic people can become sensitised, the existence of atopy cannot be used as a basis for excluding people from employment in jobs where respiratory sensitisers are used.

EXTENT OF RESPIRATORY SENSITISATION

17   The Labour Force Survey[2] estimated that 20 000 people believe they have asthma caused by substances breathed in at work. A further 50 000 believe that their asthma is made worse by work.

18   Studies in industries with a recognised risk of sensitisation revealed that up to 30% of workers had occupational asthma. However, some studies did not take into account those with asthma who were no longer exposed and so underestimate the numbers of people affected by overlooking those who had to change their job because of their asthma.

19   HSE are sponsoring researchers to run a scheme known as SWORD (Surveillance of Work-related and Occupational Respiratory Disease) which collects information on new occurrences of occupational asthma. The scheme gives an estimate of over 1000 people developing occupational asthma each year. As the scheme only includes asthma sufferers examined by participating occupational health or chest physicians it is likely to underestimate the true incidence of disease.

THE LAW REQUIRES...

20 The Control of Substances Hazardous to Health (COSHH) Regulations 1994 set out the legal requirements for protecting people in your workplace against health risks from hazardous substances which include respiratory sensitisers. Failure to comply with COSHH is an offence subject to penalties under the Health and Safety at Work etc Act 1974.

COMPLYING WITH COSHH

21 This guidance gives you the *main* provisions of the COSHH Regulations and advice on how to comply with them if exposure to respiratory sensitisers could occur in your workplace. It helps you to take account of the *particular features* of respiratory sensitisation. For more general information on COSHH, we recommend you read *COSHH: A brief guide for employers*[3] (which is free) as an introduction and the COSHH Approved Code of Practice[4].

22 To comply with COSHH you will have to:

- assess the risks to health arising from your work with hazardous substances;

- decide what precautions you need to take;

- prevent or control the risks;

- ensure the control measures are used and maintained properly;

- monitor the exposure of workers where necessary;

- provide health surveillance, as appropriate;

- inform, instruct and train employees about the risks and the precautions needed.

23 You are required by COSHH to ensure your employees' exposure to hazardous substances is either prevented or, where this is not reasonably practicable, adequately controlled. You have to try to prevent exposure first. This can be done by:

- changing the method of work so that the operation causing exposure is no longer necessary;

- modifying the process to eliminate the production of a hazardous by-product or waste product; or

- substituting an alternative substance or a different form of the same substance which presents no risk, or less risk, to health.

24 If prevention of exposure is not reasonably practicable, then you must adequately control exposure by one or other of the following measures:

- total enclosure of the process;

- partial enclosure and extraction equipment;

The processing of seafood could lead to occupational asthma

Seafood link to asthma

PRAWNS can trigger asthma attacks, according to scientists studying the high rate of respiratory problems found among workers in the seafood industry.

A survey of about 200 workers in a processsing factory found that 26 women who remove prawn shells with handheld water jets had the symptoms of asthma, such as wheezing and breathing difficulties.

The scientists discovered that the workers had inhaled a protein called tropomyosin which is found in the muscles of prawns. In 15 the protein had caused an allergy typically seen in asthma sufferers.

- systems of work and handling procedures which minimise the chances of spills, leaks and other escape of hazardous materials.

25 If this still cannot achieve adequate control, you must provide suitable personal protective equipment and ensure adequate training, instruction and supervision are given in its use.

ADEQUATE CONTROL AND EXPOSURE LIMITS

26 There are two types of exposure limit which help to decide what standards of control you are required to achieve. Maximum exposure limits (MEL) which are given in Schedule 1 of the COSHH Regulations and occupational exposure standards (OES) which are approved and published by the Health and Safety Commission. A full list of MELs and OESs is published annually in EH40 *Occupational exposure limits 1994*[5].

PRACTICAL ADVICE ON CONTROLLING RESPIRATORY SENSITISERS

27 So far we have explained what respiratory sensitisers do to people and what COSHH requires you to do to protect workers who are exposed to them. If you now turn to Annexes 1 and 2 you will find two lists of respiratory sensitisers. Annex 1 gives six groups of sensitisers which are the major causes of occupational asthma. Annex 2 lists about 40 other substances which doctors think have caused asthma in some workers. From 1995 EH40 *Occupational exposure limits* will give a list of sensitisers which have been assigned the risk phrase R42, 'may cause sensitisation by inhalation' and other substances which HSE/C have reviewed and consider to be respiratory sensitisers. This list is updated each year. You should keep these lists in mind while reading this next section which gives practical guidance on how to comply with COSHH if you use respiratory sensitisers.

28 We have set down below some of the regulations in COSHH, followed by a checklist of questions or actions for you to take and some general comments. The regulations

are legal requirements. The advice is based on good practice. There is no legal obligation on you to follow it, if you choose other ways of complying with the Regulations.

29 Your primary aim must be to prevent your employees from developing respiratory sensitisation, by assessing the risks and applying good standards of control. However, since for many sensitisers 'safe' levels of exposure are not known, health surveillance will be needed.

30 If health surveillance indicates an individual has developed sensitisation this should be confirmed by a doctor or chest physician. Normally, you will then need to make a thorough examination of the circumstances. You will need to review your COSHH assessment. This may indicate you need to take action (for example improved control measures, better instruction and training, the use of respiratory protective equipment for certain tasks) to prevent other employees from becoming sensitised. *Respiratory protective equipment, a practical guide for users*[6] and *Respiratory protective equipment, legislative requirements and lists of HSE approved standards and type approved equipment*[7] will give you further information.

ADVICE ON COMPLYING WITH THE REGULATIONS

REGULATION 6 ASSESSMENT OF HEALTH RISKS

REGULATION (in part)

(1) An employer shall not carry on any work which is liable to expose any employees to any substance hazardous to health unless he has made a suitable and sufficient assessment of the risks created by that work to the health of those employees and of the steps that need to be taken to meet the requirements of these Regulations.

(2) The assessment required by paragraph (1) shall be regularly reviewed and forthwith if -
   (a) there is reason to suspect that the assessment is no longer valid; or
   (b) there has been a significant change in the work to which the assessment relates,
and, where as a result of the review, changes in the assessment are required, those changes shall be made.

Check-list

Which respiratory sensitisers are likely to be found in your workplace?

Comment   You should refer to the list of respiratory sensitisers in Annexes 1 and 2 and information in *Occupational exposure limits*[5]. You can also get information from suppliers' safety data sheets. Remember to read the label on substances supplied to you. A number of respiratory sensitisers have been assigned the risk phrase 'may cause sensitisation by inhalation' (R 42). Other sources of information you may find useful are trade journals and information from trade associations.

Which of your activities might cause exposure to respiratory sensitisers, including occasional activities?

Consider which of your processes may cause short-term exposures much higher than the long-term average.

Consider which groups of people could be exposed.

Comment   Respiratory sensitisation may be caused by infrequent, high, short-term exposures as well as continuous exposure at lower levels. So, you should pay attention to maintenance and other staff who may get very high exposures over a short period of time.

Consider whether any exposed or potentially exposed employees have asthma and whether it could be due to a substance you use.

Comment   You should use information from health surveillance to identify individuals who may have developed respiratory sensitisation to substances used in your workplace. Your assessment will need to consider what steps to take to protect the health of such individuals. Remember even minute exposures may lead to a worsening of symptoms and chronic lung damage. To protect their health you may need to ensure exposure to the substance is eliminated. Possible options are relocation or, in some circumstances, the use of personal protective equipment.

Compare possible exposures to any occupational exposure limits.

Comment   For many respiratory sensitisers there is either limited or no information which would enable you to set an in-house exposure limit. In these circumstances reduce exposure as low as is reasonably practicable.

You must review the assessment if health surveillance indicates that an individual has become sensitised. In that case, focus on the substances the person handles, work practices and other materials that could be breathed in, including those from neighbouring workstations.

Some skin sensitisers are also respiratory sensitisers. Generally, respiratory sensitisation results from breathing in the substance and dermatitis from skin contact. In some cases skin contact may cause sensitisation, so that if the substance is subsequently breathed in, asthma may develop.

Spray painting with isocyanates - note the use of PPE

Don't forget respiratory sensitisers may have other toxic effects. For example some chemical sensitisers are respiratory irritants, others are skin sensitisers. This guidance does not cover these effects but you will need to prevent or control them as well as respiratory sensitisation.

Where respiratory protective equipment is needed, does it fully protect the wearer?

Actions

- **Decide whether exposures are likely to present a risk to health.**

- **If yes, consider the measures you should take to achieve adequate control.**

- **Determine procedure for ensuring adequate control is maintained. (If the substance does not have an occupational exposure limit you will need to determine standards of control.) Consider the seriousness of the effect in defining acceptable control levels.**

A reminder

Remember you must review the assessment if new information becomes available.

CASE STUDY

Old data sheet causes asthma

A 46-year old woman was employed by a firm that makes car door components. She worked on an assembly line, glueing rubber seals onto the back of car door handles. About three weeks after she began this work, she started getting short of breath and developed a cough in the evenings. Three months later she was admitted to hospital after a severe asthma attack at work.

The hospital physician referred the case to HSE's Employment Medical Advisory Service, who realised that the woman's problem was associated with breathing in glue at work.

Managers at the company had not carried out adequate COSHH assessments and were using a safety data sheet which was out of date. (The up-to-date sheet for the glue identified it as a respiratory sensitiser.) They were very surprised to learn that the woman's work had caused her problem. With advice from HSE, they have brought in better methods of controlling the glue vapour.

Because her condition was recognised as occupational asthma, the woman has been redeployed within the firm. Unlike many sufferers she has not had to face a drop in salary. She recovered within a few months and has been well since.

REGULATION 7   PREVENTION OR CONTROL OF EXPOSURES

REGULATION (in part)

(1) Every employer shall ensure that the exposure of his employees to substances hazardous to health is either prevented or, where this is not reasonably practicable, adequately controlled.

Check-list

Consider whether you can prevent exposure by:
- **eliminating or substituting the sensitiser;**
- **segregating work that may carry a risk of exposure.**

Comment   If you consider substitution you should take care to ensure one sensitiser is not being replaced by another. This is important where the substitute is chemically similar to the one you are replacing. Equally, you should not replace the sensitiser with a substance which presents a different but equally serious hazard to health. Your supplier, trade association or HSE may be able to give you advice.

You may be able to reduce airborne levels of a respiratory sensitiser by substituting a granular or liquid form of the substance for a finely divided powder.

If the sensitiser has an occupational exposure standard, are exposures below the standard?

Comment   For a substance with an OES, exposure by inhalation should be reduced to that standard. However, if exposure by inhalation exceeds the OES, then control will still be considered to be adequate provided you have identified why the OES has been exceeded and are taking appropriate steps to comply with the OES as soon as is reasonably practicable.

A number of occupational exposure limits for respiratory sensitisers were set to protect against toxic effects other than sensitisation. For example for some substances we did not know of the sensitisation hazard when the limit was set. We are reviewing the limits for a number of these substances. Even if you are controlling exposures to or below the OES, health surveillance is therefore likely to be appropriate. If you find that sensitisation has occurred below the OES we recommend that you reduce exposure further. If this happens, we would appreciate it if you could tell us; it would contribute to the reviews. Our address is on page 33.

If the sensitiser has a maximum exposure limit, are exposures reduced as far as reasonably practicable below the limit?

Comment   For substances with an MEL, control of exposure by inhalation is only considered adequate if exposure is reduced so far as is reasonably practicable and in any case, below the MEL.

Using a vacuum extraction system to transfer sensitising plant material. Note the use of airline breathing apparatus with hood

You should consider exposure in relation to in-house exposure limits.

Comment   For substances not assigned an MEL or an OES, control is usually considered adequate if the levels of exposure are such that most people would not develop respiratory sensitisation if exposed to the substance at that level day after day.

You may find it is not possible to control exposure to levels which will prevent symptoms in employees who have previously developed occupational asthma. Such people may suffer symptoms at very low, even undetectable, levels. However, you still have responsibilities under the COSHH Regulations to protect their health.

If you can only achieve control by the use of respiratory protective equipment, is the equipment suitable and of the appropriate standard?

Comment   If personal protective equipment is used you must take care to ensure that it is adequate. For example, a nuisance dust mask is unlikely to be effective[6,7].

CASE STUDY

Isocyanates sensitise two

Two workers from an electroplating factory had symptoms suggestive of occupational asthma. Diagnosis was confirmed by lung function tests in the workplace but no known causative agent was apparent on initial enquiries.

Subsequently one worker produced a safety data sheet describing a lacquer containing 7% isophorone diisocyanate. This lacquer was used in the workplace to coat the silver-plated goods; the lacquer was then cured in an oven.

The factory initially denied using isocyanates. However, a visit from HSE confirmed their use and tests revealed levels of isocyanate above the MEL. Testing with smoke tracer gas above the ovens revealed that the ceiling deflected contaminated air rising from the ovens back down onto the workforce. The factory has now installed extraction with a dramatic improvement in isocyanate levels. The first worker took early retirement on medical grounds and has received statutory compensation for occupational asthma due to isocyanates. The second worker has changed employment and has applied for compensation.

REGULATION 8 — USE OF CONTROL MEASURES

REGULATION (in part)

(1) Every employer who provides any control measure, personal protective equipment or other thing or facility pursuant to these Regulations shall take all reasonable steps to ensure that it is properly used or applied as the case may be.

Check-list

You must ensure your employees use the control measures correctly.

Comment   It is your responsibility to ensure that your employees are properly trained, informed and instructed in the use of the control measures. This is particularly important since sensitisers may not have irritant or other noticeable adverse effects at concentrations which can cause sensitisation.

You should check that respiratory and other protective equipment is used correctly and properly stored when not in use.

Comment   You must ensure that the equipment provided is in good working order. You can achieve this through checks at appropriate intervals. Take prompt remedial action where any defect is found.

Remember, you must take prompt remedial action if control measures or respiratory protective equipment are found to be defective.

Comment   You will need to make clear to employees the importance of reporting any defects in engineering controls or damage to respiratory protective equipment.
   You will need to take appropriate control measures during non-routine operations, such as maintenance.

CASE STUDY

Safety representative spots bakers' asthma

A 51-year old maintenance fitter had worked at a baking firm for about 20 years. He did not smoke or have any history of asthma before he started work at this firm. He complained of breathlessness, wheeze and cough which had been getting gradually worse during the past 15 years. While at work his eyes often became red and watery and he had attacks of sneezing. His symptoms were not affected by seasonal changes but he had noticed that they improved when he was away from work.
   A chest physician had previously diagnosed asthma and allergic rhinitis but did not associate the man's symptoms with his work - it was the trade union representative who suspected an occupational cause.
   A series of tests showed that his lung function was considerably better at weekends and on

Dust extraction fitted to tripledrum sander - without dust exhaust (high intensity beam photo)

Dust extraction fitted to tripledrum sander - with dust exhaust - complete and effective removal of dust

holiday. Further tests indicated a flour dust allergy.

As a result of these investigations management arranged for him to work in less dusty areas of the plant, issued him with suitable respiratory protective equipment and improved the local exhaust ventilation.

This man remains at work, using respiratory protective equipment to control exposure and extensive medication to alleviate his symptoms. However, his general respiratory health is poor because of chronic asthma, for which he receives disablement benefit. Investigations at the workplace revealed that this particular man was not the only victim - two further cases of floor dust allergy were detected. These workers have fared better because their sensitisation was recognised earlier. Even so, they still require medication to control their symptoms and are likely to suffer from respiratory problems for the rest of their lives.

REGULATION 9   MAINTENANCE, EXAMINATION AND TEST OF CONTROL MEASURES ETC

REGULATION (in part)

(1) Every employer who provides any control measure to meet the requirements of regulation 7 shall ensure that it is maintained in an efficient state, in efficient working order and in good repair.

Check-list

You will need to ensure control measures perform as originally intended.

Comment   For example, if you or your employees use respiratory protective equipment it is essential that the filters are changed regularly and that the equipment is stored so that internal surfaces do not become contaminated with the sensitiser.

You should examine and test control measures at suitable or specified intervals.

Comment   Your non-routine operations may cause a particular risk, so you should have arrangements for the maintenance, examination and testing of those control measures which:
- may only be used from time to time;
- are required during maintenance work;
- could cause high exposures if they failed.

CASE STUDY

Glue cripples sportsman

A 41-year old night shift worker with a rubber company was concerned that his work caused his attacks of breathlessness. They had gradually become more severe until he could not walk more than 150 yards on the flat without panting.

The worker said that he had been employed for a year on a machine that sprayed an isocyanate-containing glue onto extruded rubber. Before this episode of illness, he had been fit and healthy and played football regularly. Although he smoked, he had never suffered with asthma or any other lung trouble.

Investigation of the man's workplace showed that spraying took place in a fully automated spray booth equipped with local

Colophony fumes - the absence of any extraction results in operator breathing in the fumes

exhaust ventilation. *The air flow across the opening of the booth was adequate but joints around a fan casing were leaking, as was an inadequately sealed inspection cover.* No other source for the isocyanate exposure was found.

A chest physician diagnosed asthma associated with exposure to isocyanates. Following the incident the offending seals and joints were repaired and a programmed schedule of maintenance undertaken. The affected individual was transferred from that area of the plant and given work elsewhere on site. However, as well as losing money because of transfer from night shift to day shift, his health remains poor, he suffers from chronic asthma and can no longer participate in the sporting activities he once enjoyed.

REGULATION 10   MONITORING EXPOSURE AT THE W

REGULATION (in part)

(1) In any case in which -
(a) it is requisite for ensuring the maintenance of adequate control of the exposure of employees to substances hazardous to health; or
(b) it is otherwise requisite for protecting the health of employees, the employer shall ensure that the exposure of employees to substances hazardous to health is monitored in accordance with a suitable procedure.

Check-list

Remember, you may need to carry out monitoring if your employees are exposed to respiratory sensitisers.

Comment   Monitoring is not a substitute for adequate control, but may be required to ensure that control is adequate.

Monitoring exposure of your employees to respiratory sensitisers should preferably be by measurement of personal exposures and tailored to the needs identified in the COSHH assessment.

For many of the naturally occurring respiratory sensitisers (for example flour dust) specific monitoring methods are not available. In these circumstances you can use total dust measurements as a surrogate measure of sensitiser concentration. However, remember the sensitiser may be a small and variable proportion of the total dust. For these materials it may not be enough to keep total inhalable dust below the 'guidance value' of 10 mg m^{-3} (see *Occupational exposure limits*[5] and the COSHH General ACOP[4]).

To provide useful information on personal exposure your monitoring programmes need to be closely aligned with work patterns to ensure that peaks of exposure are measured as well as long-term exposures.

Grain being discharged from silos

REGULATION 11   HEALTH SURVEILLANCE

REGULATION (in part)

(1) Where it is appropriate for the protection of the health of his employees who are, or are liable to be, exposed to substances hazardous to health, the employer shall ensure that such employees are under suitable health surveillance.

(2) Health surveillance shall be treated as being appropriate where -
(b) the exposure of the employee to a substance hazardous to health is such that an identifiable disease or adverse health effect may be related to the exposure, there is a reasonable likelihood that the disease or effect may occur under the particular conditions of his work and there are valid techniques for detecting indications of the disease or the effect.

Check-list

Remember that health surveillance is appropriate for all employees significantly exposed to respiratory sensitisers.

Remember the level of health surveillance must be related to the degree of risk of developing sensitisation.

Comment   Health surveillance is appropriate for all your employees who may be exposed to respiratory sensitisers unless the COSHH assessment has shown that there is unlikely to be a risk of sensitisation under the conditions of use.
We recommend three levels of health surveillance:

- Where there is only limited evidence of a hazard and limited exposure you should carry out a low level of health surveillance. You should find out about past or present symptoms of respiratory sensitivity (for baseline information only). You should also tell employees about the symptoms to watch for and advise them to report such symptoms to an identified responsible person.
- Where there is more positive evidence of a hazard, for example the substance is included in the list of sensitisers in Annex 2, you should introduce a system of enquiry, positively seeking evidence of symptoms among your employees. The enquiries may be carried out by a properly trained responsible person in accordance with the instructions of an occupational health doctor or nurse who should be involved in training the responsible person and setting up the surveillance system. A screening questionnaire that can be used by the responsible person is given in Annex 3. Any symptoms which suggest respiratory sensitisation reported to or identified by the responsible person should be referred immediately to the doctor or nurse for further investigation. Responsible persons should not be expected to make judgements about the cause of symptoms.

- Where there is a high degree of hazard, for example your employees may be exposed to substances on the list in Annex 1, a higher level of surveillance is necessary. In addition to the measures above, this is likely to include pre-exposure assessments by an occupational health professional and lung function tests as appropriate. A system of regular examinations by a doctor or occupational health nurse may be appropriate.

You may wish to seek advice from an occupational health professional on the level of health surveillance appropriate for your workplace and in setting up the procedures.

You should provide suitable facilities to enable the surveillance team to carry out their tasks. When certain tasks require more sophisticated equipment the use of specialised units (such as teaching hospitals) may be necessary. The level of surveillance should be related to the degree of risk identified during the COSHH assessment.

Further guidance on health surveillance is given in *Medical aspects of occupational asthma*[8] and *Health surveillance under COSHH*[9].

A reminder

- **Health surveillance is not a substitute for preventing or adequately controlling exposure but is an additional requirement to protect your employees' health.**
- **Your surveillance will need to include the maintenance of a health record for each exposed individual.**

REGULATION 12 INFORMATION, INSTRUCTION AND TRAINING

REGULATION (in part)

(1) An employer who undertakes work which may expose any of his employees to substances hazardous to health shall provide that employee with such information, instruction and training as is suitable and sufficient for him to know-
   (a) the risks to health created by such exposure; and
   (b) the precautions which should be taken.

Check-list

You should inform employees about:
- the substances to which they are exposed;
- typical symptoms of respiratory sensitisation;
- the need to report such symptoms;
- the arrangements for health surveillance;
- the irreversibility of sensitisation; and
- the risks of long-term breathing difficulties if exposure continues once sensitisation has occurred so that they understand the need to attend for health surveillance.

Your employees will need to understand both the importance of control measures to prevent them coming into contact with respiratory sensitisers and how to use those measures.

Comment   You will need to impress upon your employees the consequences to their health of respiratory sensitisation and therefore the need to use the control measures provided.
   We have published an information card which you can give to your employees[10]. Information may also be available from trade associations and manufacturers.

CASE STUDY

Ignorance of anhydrides causes handicap

A 30-year old man was employed in a plastics processing company. His job was to mix batches of ingredients, supplied in granular form, for subsequent processing. After some time he began to notice increasing nose and eye discomfort at work. This became associated with chest tightness and wheezing, which came on several hours after work. He would wake up at night wheezing and fighting for breath. His physical fitness deteriorated steadily. This particularly worried him because he had been an extremely keen athlete until this point.

His doctor referred him to a chest physician, who contacted HSE, as it appeared that his symptoms might have an occupational cause. Investigation of his job and the substances he used at work led to investigation of a cross linking agent used in plastics coatings, which was supplied in sacks. The supplier advised that the agent contained an acid anhydride.

Although managers in the company were aware of health problems associated with anhydrides, they did not have a current data sheet and no information, instruction and training had been given to workers.

The man was investigated more fully in hospital and occupational asthma due to exposure to anhydrides was diagnosed. He was advised to avoid further exposure. The consequences of respiratory sensitisation have been devastating for him. After four years away from exposure he is still unemployed and his level of physical fitness has grossly deteriorated.

ANNEXES

ANNEX 1 SUBSTANCES RESPONSIBLE FOR MOST CASES OF OCCUPATIONAL ASTHMA*

Substance groups	*Examples of substances*	*Common activities*
Isocyanates	TDI[†] MDI[†] HDI[†]	coach and other spray painting; foam manufacturing
Flour/grain/hay	flour barley wheat oats maize rye	handling grain at docks; milling, malting, baking
Soldering flux	colophony fume	welding, soldering, electronic assembly
Laboratory animals	urine/dander from laboratory animals	laboratory animal work
Wood dusts	African teak (Iroko) western red cedar	sawmilling, woodworking
Glues/resins	PA[‡] TCPA[‡] TMA[‡] MA[‡] MTPA[‡]	curing of epoxy resins

Notes

* Information obtained from SWORD scheme - see paragraph 19

† TDI = toluene-2,4-diisocyanate
MDI = diphenylmethane-diisocyanate
HDI = hexamethylene-diisocyanate

‡ PA = phthalic anhydride
TCPA = tetrachlophthalic anhydride
TMA = trimellitic anhydride
MA = maleic anhydride
MTPA = methyltetrahydrophthalic anhydride

ANNEX 2 SOME OTHER SUBSTANCES REPORTED TO CAUSE RESPIRATORY SENSITISATION*

Antibiotics
ampicillins
cephalosporins
penicillins

Inorganic substances (as salts)
chromium
cobalt
nickel
platinum

Organic substances
azodicarbonamide
carmine
chloramine T
cyanoacrylates
diazonium salts
ethylenediamine
glutaraldehyde
hydralazine
persulphate salts
piperazine
certain reactive dyes
spiramycin

Proteolytic enzymes
amylase
bromolein
cellulase
papain
subtilisins
xylanase

Substances of animal origin
cockroaches
cow epithelium/urine
crustacean proteins
egg proteins
pancreatic extracts
pig epithelium/urine
storage mites

Substances of plant or microbial origin
castor bean dust
green coffee bean dust
guar gum
henna
ispaghula (psyllium)
latex
mist from oil-in-water cutting fluids
    (*Pseudomonas* bacteria)
soybean dust
tea dust

Note
* Most of these substances are currently being reviewed. An up-to-date list of respiratory sensitisers will be published annually in EH40 *Occupational exposure limits* from 1995.

ANNEX 3 SAMPLE QUESTIONNAIRES FOR SURVEILLANCE OF EMPLOYEES WORKING WITH RESPIRATORY SENSITISERS

This is a suggested format for a questionnaire which could be used by a responsible person as part of health surveillance and may be reproduced freely. The questionnnaire has been tried out to a limited extent, and we would appreciate comments on its use. Individual occupational health professionals may wish to modify it to suit their local circumstances.

These questionnaires are intended for use by responsible persons as part of health surveillance programmes for workers exposed to respiratory sensitisers.

The responsible person should be properly trained in accordance with the instructions of an occupational health doctor or nurse who should be involved in setting up the surveillance system. All symptoms indicative of respiratory sensitisation reported should be referred immediately to the doctor or nurse for further investigation. Responsible persons should not be expected to make judgements on the cause of the symptoms.

Notes for the responsible person:
1. Employees should be instructed about the possible effects of sensitisation and should be warned that symptoms can occur outside working hours.
2. The pre-exposure questionnaire should be administered prior to commencing work to establish health status.
3. While work with respiratory sensitisers continues the periodic questionnaire should be used at six weeks, six months and annually thereafter, or as advised by the occupational health adviser to the company.
4. Employees exposed to respiratory sensitisers who develop any symptoms indicative of respiratory sensitisation should be referred to the company occupational health adviser for further investigation.

Initial questionnaire for surveillance of persons who will be working with known respiratory sensitisers

To be completed by the responsible person

Company name _____

Address _____

_____

_____

In this workplace substances are in use which have been known to cause allergic chest problems. Following the risk assessment under the Control of Substances Hazardous to Health 1994 (COSHH) Regulation 6, management have decided to carry out a programme of pre-exposure and periodic health surveillance COSHH 1994 Reg 11 (2b).

In some cases further advice may be required from the company occupational health adviser.

I understand that a programme of health surveillance is necessary in this employment and will form part of my management health record.

Signature of employee _____ Date _____

Signature of responsible person _____ Date _____

Referred for further investigation ☐

Would you please answer the following questions:

1 Surname _____ Forenames _____

   Date of birth _____

   Home address _____

   _____

   _____

   Tel number _____

2 Have you any chest problems, such as periods of breathlessness, wheeze, chest tightness or persistent coughing? Yes ☐ No ☐

3 Do you believe that your chest has suffered as a result of any previous employment? Yes ☐ No ☐

4 Do you or have you ever had any of the following? (Do not include isolated colds, sore throats or flu)

    (a) Recurring soreness of or watering of eyes Yes ☐ No ☐

    (b) Recurring blocked or running nose Yes ☐ No ☐

    (c) Bouts of coughing Yes ☐ No ☐

    (d) Chest tightness Yes ☐ No ☐

    (e) Wheezing Yes ☐ No ☐

    (f) Breathlessness Yes ☐ No ☐

    (g) Any other persistent or history of chest problems Yes ☐ No ☐

To be completed by the responsible person

    (a) No further action required ☐

    (b) Refer to company occupational health adviser ☐

Signed (responsible person) _____ Date _____

I confirm that the responses given by me are correct and that I have received a copy of the completed questionnaire.

Signed _____ Date _____

Health questionnaire for on-going surveillance of persons working with respiratory sensitisers

To be completed by the responsible person

Employee's name _____ Works no _____

The questionnaire should be completed six weeks, six months and annually after employment commences or as advised by the company occupational health adviser.

Further advice will be required from the company occupational health adviser if any yes box is ticked.

Since starting your present job have you had any of the following symptoms either at work or at home? (Do not include isolated colds, sore throats or flu)

(a) Recurring soreness of or watering of eyes   Yes ☐ No ☐

(b) Recurring blocked or running nose   Yes ☐ No ☐

(c) Bouts of coughing   Yes ☐ No ☐

(d) Chest tightness   Yes ☐ No ☐

(e) Wheeze   Yes ☐ No ☐

(f) Breathlessness   Yes ☐ No ☐

(g) Have you consulted your doctor about chest problems since the last questionnaire?   Yes ☐ No ☐

To be completed by the responsible person

(a) No further action required   ☐

(b) Refer to company occupational health adviser   ☐

Signature of responsible person _____ Date _____

I confirm that the responses given by me are correct and that I have received a copy of the completed questionnaire.

Signed _____ Date _____

ANNEX 4 REFERENCES AND FURTHER READING

1   Occupational respiratory disease in the United Kingdom 1989: a report to the British Thoracic Society and the Society of Occupational Medicine by the SWORD project group *British Journal of Industrial Medicine* 1991 48: 292-298
SK Meredith, VM Taylor and JC McDonald*

2   *Self-reported work-related illness. Results from a trailer questionnaire on the 1990 Labour Force Survey in England and Wales* Research Paper No 33 1993
HSE Books JT Hodgson, JR Jones, RC Elliot and J Osman (eds)**
ISBN 0 7176 0607 4

3   *COSHH: A brief guide for employers: The requirements of the Control of Substances Hazardous to Health (COSHH) Regulations 1988* 1993 HSE Books IND(G) 136L

4   *Control of Substances Hazardous to Health and Control of Carcinogenic Substances. Control of Substances Hazardous to Health Regulations 1988. Approved Codes of Practice.* (COSHH General ACOP) L5 (4th ed) 1993 HSE Books
ISBN 0 7176 0427 6

5   EH 40/94 *Occupational exposure limits 1994*

6   HS(G)53 *Respiratory protective equipment, a practical guide for users*
1990 HSE Books ISBN 0 11 885522 0

7   *Respiratory protective equipment, legislative requirements and lists of HSE-approved standards and type-approved equipment* 1992 HSE Books ISBN 0 11 886382 7

8   MS 25 *Medical aspects of occupational asthma* 1991 HSE Books
ISBN 0 11 885584 0

9   HS(G) 61 *Surveillance of people exposed to health risks at work* 1990 HSE Books
ISBN 0 11 885574 3

10 *Breathe freely - a workers' information card on respiratory sensitisers* IND(G) 172L
1994 HSE ISBN 0 7176 0771 2 (available in packs of 25 from HSE Books)

*   The surveillance of work-related and occupational respiratory disease (SWORD) is an HSE-sponsored voluntary scheme established in 1989 and run by the Epidemiological Research Unit at the National Heart and Lung Institute, London. It receives reports from chest physicians and occupational physicians representing up to 90% of the chest clinics in the country. Nevertheless, it is estimated that the true incidence of acute occupational respiratory disease is three times higher than that reported.

** The Labour Force Survey (LFS) is part of an overall programme aimed at providing a better statistical base on the scale of occupational disease. Information was collected on individuals' perception of the relationship between their work and their health in a 'trailer' to the 1990 LFS.

   Data were collected from a representative national sample of some 75 000 adults in England and Wales who were asked whether, in the last year, they had suffered from any illness which in their opinion was caused or made worse by their work.

If you have any comments on this guidance or would like to give us any feedback, please contact:

> The Secretariat
> Working Group on the Assessment of Toxic Chemicals
> Health and Safety Executive
> Health Policy Division
> Rose Court
> 2 Southwark Bridge Road
> London SE1 9HF

You may obtain further help on the issues discussed in this publication from:

1. HSE Area Offices (see Yellow Pages)

2. Offices of the Local Authority Environmental Health Department (see Yellow pages)

3. Trade Associations (see Yellow Pages)

4. HSE Information Centre
   Broad Lane
   Sheffield S3 7HQ
   Tel: 0742 892345
   Fax: 0742 892333

Printed and published by the Health and Safety Executive   C200   4/94

QUESTIONNAIRE

We would very much like to have your views on this publication. Please complete this tear-off slip and return it to The Secretariat, Working Group on the Assessment of Toxic Chemicals, Health and Safety Executive, Health Policy Division, Rose Court, 2 Southwark Bridge Road, London SE1 9HF. The first 2000 people to return the questionnaire will receive ten workers' cards.

Are you

☐ an employer? ☐ an employee? ☐ self-employed?

☐ trade union representative? ☐ occupational physician?

☐ company health and safety representative?

☐ member of the public?

How many people work in your firm?

☐ 1-24 ☐ 25-49 ☐ 50-99 ☐ 100+

What industrial activity are you involved in?
_____

_____

What substances do you use in your work?
_____

_____

_____

How useful was this booklet to you?

☐ extremely useful? ☐ very useful? ☐ not useful enough? ☐ useless?

Which sections did you find most helpful?
_____

_____

_____

What improvements would you like to see?
_____

_____

_____

Please print your mailing address to receive your ten workers' cards (if eligible).
_____

_____